"Can I stay in today Miss?"
— Improving the School Playground

Ideas and Issues developed from work with Islington schools

By Carol Ross & Amanda Ryan

Acknowledgements

We would like to thank the following schools and individuals for their participation and contributions.

The Islington Schools Environment Project
Catherine Kennally, Director of Isledon Teachers' Centre
Gael Parfitt, Evaluation Consultant for ILEA
Pete Sanders, Primary Advisor for Personal, Social and Health Education
Carry Gorney of Inter-Action
Tom Leindorfer and Sue Bowers from Quaker Peace and Service and the Friends Workshop Group

Participating Schools

Ambler School
Charles Lamb School
Hargrave Park School
Highbury Quadrant School
Hugh Myddelton Junior School
Laycock School
Pakeman School
Prior Weston School
Ring Cross School
Robert Blair School
Rotherfield School
St Johns C.E. School
St Marks C.E. School
Tufnell Park School

tb

Trentham Books
151 Etruria Road, Stoke-on-Trent,
Staffordshire ST1 5NS

First published in 1990 by Trentham Books

Trentham Books
151 Etruria Road
Stoke-on-Trent
Staffordshire
England ST1 5NS

British Library Cataloguing in Publication Data

Ross, Carol
    Can I stay in today, Miss: Improving the school playground
    1. Playground. Safety aspects
    I. Title
    363.1'4

    ISBN 0-948080-42-6

Photo credits:
Amanda Ryan, pages 5,6,7,10,17,19,22,28,30,31, 39,48,52,53,55,56,57,59,66,69.
David Stone, pages 27,36,42,43,49,50,74.
Patrick Allan, pages 29,44,51,54,62.
Dave Cashman, page 46.
Fiona Keating, page 76.

Designed and Typeset by The Design Bureau, Chester
Printed in Great Britain by BPCC Wheatons Ltd, Exeter

Table of Contents

SECTION 1: WHAT ARE THE ISSUES?

Introduction

1. Background to the work

At least a fifth of the school day is spent in the playground. Yet it is often the only part of the school day which is unstructured, lacking in resources and devoid of educational aims. However, playtime is an important — sometimes over-riding — aspect of children's experience of school. Parents often comment that when they ask their children 'how was school today?' they are told a tale of the playground.

Many primary schools have identified the playground as an area of concern. They are looking at ways of developing playtime as a positive educational experience. Teachers worry that the 'hidden curriculum' in the playground (aggression, bullying and name calling, domination of play space, choice of activity, and other aspects of playground dynamics) has racist and sexist implications which go against school policy.

Incidents at playtime may carry over into the classroom and the reverse. 'Playground culture' may undermine teacher initiatives.

As the Divisional Equal Opportunities Coordinator and Advisory teacher for the Islington School Environmental Project, we were particularly concerned with the relationship between the playground and children's educational experiences. Over the past two years, we have organised a series of workshops which have explored a range of playground issues. Schools have shared experiences, ideas and strategies. Contributions were made by consultants and organisations with specialist skills and knowledge in related areas. Participating schools received support for their playground development. This handbook is an outcome of this work.

The most central point to arise from our work with schools is that in order to effect any real change in the playground, problems need to be tackled on a variety of levels. Working with children on the ways they relate to each other in the playground is an important element, but insufficient in itself.

To support fair play and equal access the play space will have to be physically changed and play activities restructured. A school policy for playtime (rules and procedures) needs to be agreed in consultation with pupils, staff and parents. Improving the playground has to be a whole school project, involving the whole school community.

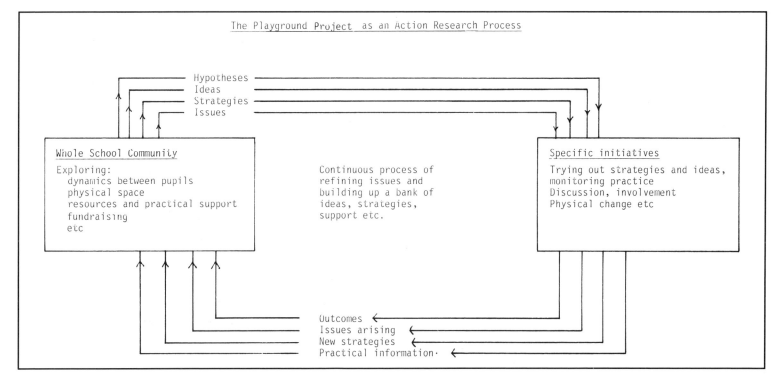

The Playground Project as an Action Research Process

BULLYING ON THE PLAYGROUND AS A WHOLE SCHOOL ISSUE

Bullying and harassment on the playground do not stand apart from other whole school issues. Work in this area needs to relate very closely to institutional policy. Bullying does not only affect the individuals involved. There are specific individuals involved in any incident and they must be dealt with — victims *must* be protected, and bullies must be confronted. But the effect of bullying extends beyond the victim-bully level. Bullying affects all children, not just those in an extreme position. It is an expression of the system of power relationships which are operating and of the corresponding value system.

In an atmosphere of 'might is right', children may seek to gain status from acts of aggression or displays of power. Many children collude in group bullying in order to escape becoming targets themselves. Other children not directly involved in bullying incidents must nonetheless find ways of operating which fit in with the tone and 'law' of the playground. In a difficult playground environment, children may adopt behaviour which is overtly aggressive (e.g. picking/starting fights) or extremely passive (e.g. staying at the edges of the playground) as ways of negotiating the situation.

Changing playground dynamics requires a holistic approach, reviewing the messages and values of the hidden school curriculum.. This means analysing the sense of school community. In order to work towards developing a school environment which promotes caring, sharing behaviour in pupils, aspects of school life need to be explored, both within and outside the classroom. For instance:

Teaching methodology

The extent that pupils are expected to work in individual or collaborative ways or are encouraged to be competitive or cooperative may effect their interactions and attitudes to one another.

Modes of discipline

Working towards fostering self discipline and collective responsibility, rather than through authoritarianism, can encourage children to develop a sense of fairness.

Status within school hierarchy

It is important that children perceive the non-teaching staff to be awarded the same respect as teachers in order to combat the notion that some people matter less than others and can be treated with less consideration.

Staff relationships

A staff which is seen by pupils to collaborate (as opposed to working completely in isolation) can offer a strong model of people working together for a common good.

Parents' role

Parental involvement at school can be a unifying influence between the values of home and school, so combating the notion that these are two separate realms, with the playground as a world unto itself.

III. Issues — Areas of Concern Relating to Equal Opportunities

Racism in The Playground

Power relationships abound in the playground and reflect those in general society. Although many schools have worked hard to develop and implement their anti-racist policies, there is much evidence of racism in the playground. Name-calling, in particular, highlights this. Our research has shown that name-calling is overwhelmingly and explicitly racist and/or sexist and is a constant feature of playtime. Racism is often operating as an on-going dimension of playground interaction. Additionally, some children are the victims of explicit racist attack. Another expression of racism in the playground is the way that racist stereotypes (often in relation to gender stereotypes), can affect the ways children are perceived and responded to. Such expectations can lead to children absorbing or internalising these negative images. Two common examples are the extreme stereotypes relating to Asian girls as quiet and passive and to Black boys as aggressive.

Girls and Boys in The Playground

Schools are concerned with ensuring equal opportunities for both girls and boys. However, our work revealed that in the playground, girls and boys are usually engaged in different sorts of activities and may be treated differently. Play space is often dominated by a group of boys (for example, playing football). Even active 'girls' games', such as skipping or hopscotch, are played within a more confined space. Girls often find themselves vulnerable to disruption or deliberate intimidation over such things as boundaries or ownership of an activity. The marginalisation of girls to the edges of the playground is both the result and a defensive action.

Girls in The Playground

Girls are often given 'double messages' which affect their self-image, behaviour and expectations.

Girls may, for instance, be complimented about 'looking nice', but their clothes and shoes can restrict them in their activities. After an upsetting incident, we have seen girls comforted and encouraged to remain with the adult, in contrast to the adult taking boys back to the group and 'sorting it out'. Differences in the ways we respond to girls and boys give strong messages about what is expected of them. In this case, girls are learning to 'opt out' of an active role.

Girls are often being asked to 'understand' the boys' point of view and sacrifice their own needs in conflicts over use of space or ownership of an activity. The following incidents are typical:

1. **Three girls playing on the painted hopscotch game:** A group of boys wanted to play football on the neighbouring pitch and decided they needed that area as well. A conflict ensues. The girls are asked to give ;up their game because the boys need the space.

2. **Five girls playing a skipping game:** They are asked to allow a boy to join them because he has been pushed out of a football game. The girls object but are 'talked into' accepting him into their game.

In both incidents, the girls were being relied on to be the reasonable party. They were asked to accommodate the boys' needs above their own. Furthermore, they were given the clear (if unspoken) message that this is an expected part of being 'nice'. These examples were not uncommon but we never observed boys being treated in this way.

Below: Many games girls play use litle space.
Bottom: Girls playing on the edges of the playground still face disruption.

Boys in the Playground

Boys are under different pressures. For many boys, the playground becomes a 'proving ground' for their masculinity. Being physically strong, being good at sports, not showing 'softness', etc can be the pre-requisite for acceptance. This can be damaging whether or not a boy is able to fit into this model of behaviour. For those who cannot, it can lead to loss of status, persecution or constant ridicule. For boys who can operate in this way, it may be extremely limiting to their personal development. It leads to, 'getting into trouble' and continuous negative response from the adults in the school.

The Excluded Child

Some children are excluded as a result of the dynamics of a particular group situation. Others are consistently excluded. Excluded children may react by removing themselves or 'hiding' — avoiding playtime by asking to stay in or even not coming to school. Other children gave exclusion as the main reason that they would behave disruptively. Parents interviewed gave exclusion from friendship groups as one of the main reasons why their children were reluctant to go to school.

The problem of exclusion relates to the boredom of the playground. If there are few activities and games on offer, children find it difficult to join in with something else. The dynamics and relationships within the group become the focus rather than the activity. In a more activities-orientated playground situation, children are less compelled to negotiate themselves into a group situation.

Other Considerations

Younger children, bilingual children and children with special needs all need to be considered when evaluating power relationships on the playground. Any individual child who is 'different' in some way or who can't afford to dress in the favoured fashion can be a target for bullying.

This handbook suggests some ideas to combat inequalities and to improve the playground experience for all children.

Below: Football often dominates the playground

SECTION 2: WORKING WITH PUPILS

Classroom work and monitoring ideas with pupils

These classroom-based activities for exploring playground issues with pupils, have been developed within schools. They aim to help children to identify some problems on the playground and to enable them to discuss them openly and explore why they happen.

They are intended also to start children devising alternative strategies for coping on the playground and promote cooperative behaviour. Also included are some samples of pupils' work.

Playground issues are complex and can seem overwhelming. They involve the whole school community. Obviously children can't change playground dynamics by themselves. However, classroom work is not only an important aspect of a playground project, it can provide a starting point in developing a whole school policy and making changes.

Identifying ways to improve the playground

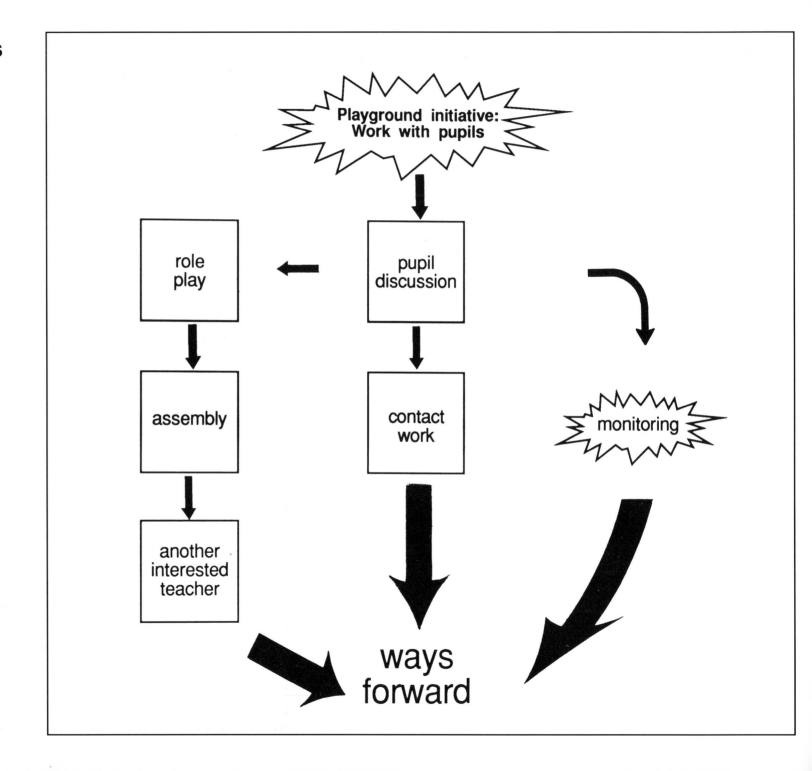

Initial Questionnaire for Pupils

The questionnaire is intended to stimulate discussion about the playground and raise issues. It could be used as a starting point for agreeing on a playtime code of conduct.

1   Pupils fill in questionnaire individually

2   In groups, pupils compare and discuss their responses. The main points are recorded.

3   Each group reports back the main points of the group discussion to the whole class.

4   From the points raised, the class can:

    a)   discuss basis for a code of conduct

    b)   select areas to investigate further

Questions about the playground

1 What do you do in the playground?

2 Who do you play with at playtime?

3 What do you like about playtime?

4 What don't you like about playtime?

5 What upsets you at playtime?

6 What causes trouble at playtime?

7 Is there bullying on the playground?

8 What do you do if there is fighting?

Trigger Cards

The trigger cards are based on what children have said about their experiences on the playground. They have been used to raise issues and generate discussion.

1   Cut into cards. Leave some blank.

2   In groups, ask pupils to rank the cards according to a set criterion (e.g. 'what happens most often?'; 'what is most true of yourself?')

3   Invite children to fill in the blank cards with their own statements

4   Share as a whole class

Trigger Cards:

What we like about the playground

"I like playing because you can shout without getting told off"	"I like playtime because you can run about and let yourself go"
"I like to play with my friends in other classes"	"At playtime, you can talk freely"
"I like the quiet playground because it is safer"	"I like playing with my friend"
"I like playing 'had' "	"I like playing with small children"

Trigger Cards:

What starts trouble on the playground

"People arguing and swearing at each other makes trouble on the playground"	"Trouble starts when people call each other names"
"Sometimes on the playground, somebody wants to start a fight"	"Football causes trouble on the playground"
"Being bullied"	"If you're left out, it makes you feel angry and you want to start a fight"
"If someone insults your family or your clothes, it might start a fight"	"Being called a 'softie' makes you want to fight"

Trigger Cards:

How we feel about bullying on the playground

"Bullying spoils your playtime"	"Bullying makes you feel like not wanting to go out to play"
"People bully to make themselves seem tough or to get revenge"	"Sometimes people don't realise what they're saying and that it could hurt the person they're speaking to"
"What upsets me at playtime is people bullying you and not letting you play"	"I get upset when people call me names or make fun of me"
"I don't like fighting. It's violent; it's stupid"	

Name Calling

Name calling is a major factor in playground conflict. Often it is explicitly racist and sexist and so should not be tolerated. Schools need to devise an agreed code of practice for dealing with name calling.

Classroom work on name calling can be a way of working with children on this issue. It can also help in the establishment of a playground policy.

1. **Survey of name calling**
   Children need to devise a survey sheet. It should be based on categories or types of name calling rather than examples or quotations so that it provides a means of analysing and examining insults without "allowing" children to insult each other. (see example1 below)

2. **Opinion Board**
   A central question (e.g **What should we do about name calling?** or **Why name calling hurts people**) is pinned up in the middle of a notice board. Children pin up their comments or feelings anonymously over a agreed period: a week or even a term (see example 2).

3. **Written Work**
   Children do creative writing on aspects of name calling (see example 3).

4. **Interviews**
   Children work in pairs, interviewing each other about issues relating to name calling (this needn't be recorded). The teacher keeps time so that interviewers and interviewee swap roles half way.

5. **Making a Contract**
   This entails children as groups deciding on and making a commitment to a set of rules or proceedings in regard to name calling.

6. **Class discussions**
   Children explore ways in which they can support each other in the playground as well as the classroom.

Example 1

A survey of name calling in the playground

Please tick

Racist	Weight	Height	Clothes	Family	Religion	Language	Speech	Face	Hair

Key
Red Class
Yellow Class
Blue Class
Green Class
Brown Class
Pink Class

Opinion Board

Example 2

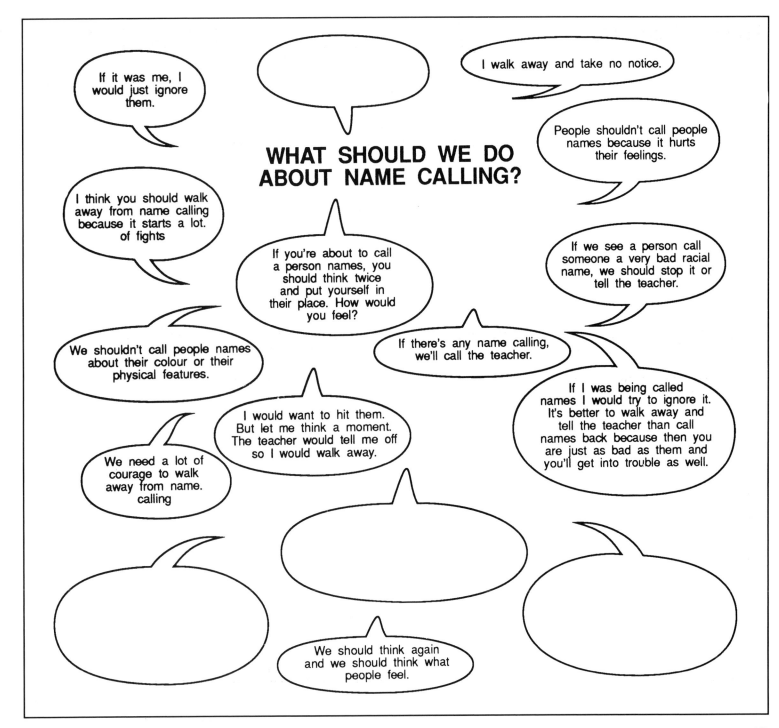

WHAT SHOULD WE DO ABOUT NAME CALLING?

If it was me, I would just ignore them.

I walk away and take no notice.

People shouldn't call people names because it hurts their feelings.

I think you should walk away from name calling because it starts a lot. of fights

If you're about to call a person names, you should think twice and put yourself in their place. How would you feel?

If we see a person call someone a very bad racial name, we should stop it or tell the teacher.

We shouldn't call people names about their colour or their physical features.

If there's any name calling, we'll call the teacher.

I would want to hit them. But let me think a moment. The teacher would tell me off so I would walk away.

If I was being called names I would try to ignore it. It's better to walk away and tell the teacher than call names back because then you are just as bad as them and you'll get into trouble as well.

We need a lot of courage to walk away from name. calling

We should think again and we should think what people feel.

Why do people call each other names?

Why do people call each other names?

Example 3

This is what one child wrote:

We call each other names because it makes us sound tough and hard and because we like to boss people about. Sometimes we don't mean it. It could hurt someone a lot. Sometimes they cry and you get into trouble. Then that makes it worse because it starts a fight and people start quarrelling and picking on each other all the time.

Sometimes, though, we do it for fun, but we have to check that they are going along with it.

Exploring Conflict

Situations for Role Play

Here is a worksheet which one school used to facilitate the role play about problems children may have in the playground. The situations were identified through classroom discussions. The aim of the role play situations was to help children devise alternative ways of dealing with playground conflict.

Here are some situations you may face on the playground. In small groups, try acting them out. Try each one several times. Find out all the different things that could happen by responding to the situation in different ways.

1. Someone insults your family

2. Someone insults your clothes

3. Someone takes your ball

4. Someone tries to make you fight

6. Someone is threatening or frightening you

7. You're left out

8. Someone is calling you names

9. You want to call the teacher, but you're afraid to

Investigating Playground Activities

An activity chart is designed to find out what games are being played by which children in the playground. Children brainstorm all the games they know to be played in the playground. These are then written as a list. Girls use a tick and boys a cross when filling in the chart. (see example 1)

Children can then use this information to produce a graph (see example 2). In a whole school survey, it is important to indicate the children's ages.

Example 1: Choose four things that you like doing.

singing		skipping		climbing	
talking		chasing		balancing	
sitting		ball games		sliding	
watching		football		swinging	
hiding		oxo, hopscotch, snakes and ladders		jumping	

Example 2: A graph showing what games are played in the playground

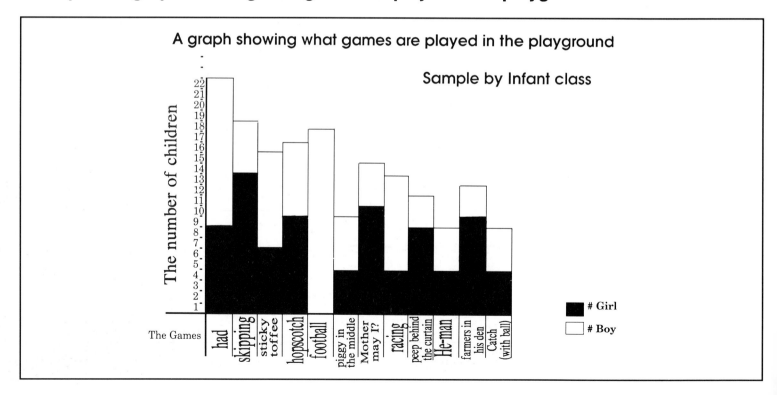

Home Games/School Games

It can be useful to find out what children play at home. Not only can it reveal a lot about the children and give them the opportunity to show their home experiences, but can also provide a rich source of new activities for the active and quiet play spaces.

This has been organised in various ways. For example:-

☐ Class brainstorm — 'games we play at home'

☐ Diary of home play

☐ Piece of writing

☐ Bringing in small toys, games etc.

Follow up questions to raise with children:-

☐ What games/activities do you like to play at home but don't like doing at school? (e.g. football) — why?

☐ What can you do at school that you can't do at home? — why?

☐ What do you play at home that is suitable for playtime at school?

☐ What games did your parents play as children? (in what country?) — grandparents?

Other Playground Users

Involving pupils in change to the playground must include making them aware of the needs of other people/groups who will be affected. Below is a worksheet that was designed to help children think about other playground users. On the next page is a worksheet to help children monitor who is using the playground at different times of the day.

People who use the playground	How they use the playground
Nursery children	
School children	
Play Centre	
Other organisations	
Parents	
Support services (eg dinner van, maintainance, school keeper etc)	

Monitoring Sheet — Who Uses The Playground

Children can use this worksheet to help them investigate who else uses the playground (before school, before lunch, at home time and after school).

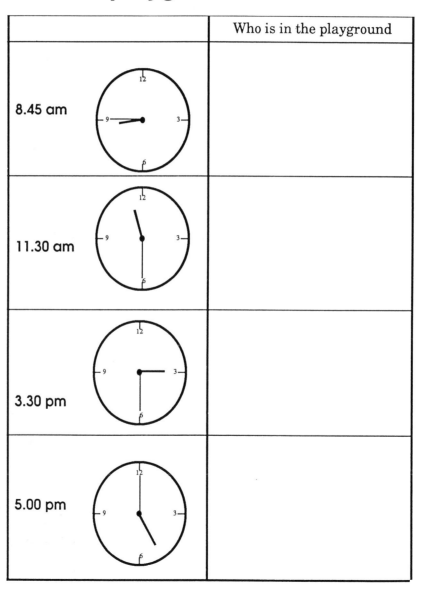

A day in the life of a playground at .... school

	Who is in the playground
8.45 am	
11.30 am	
3.30 pm	
5.00 pm	

Other People's Views

Helping pupils to investigate the playground needs to include encouraging them to find out about other people's experiences, views and feelings.

Interviewing is a useful technique for enabling children to do this. It is most effective when children take full responsibility for designing their own interview schedule and organising the whole process. They may interview playground supervisors, parents, school keeper, other children, teachers, or play centre staff.

On the following page is an example of an interview schedule devised by 4th year juniors for use with infant children.

Issues pupils needs to consider:

Skills the interviewer needs

Ways of recording the interview

Deciding on relevant questions

Setting up the interview

Should it be confidential?

Purpose of the interview

How the information collected will be used

Example: Survey with infants by top juniors

Small children in the playground

Name..

	YES	NO
do you play with older children?		
do you hate older children?		
do you cry a lot?		
do you sit alone?		
do you play with your friends?		
do you run a lot?		
do you sit quietly a lot?		
do you like older children?		
do you play football?		
do you play skipping?		
do you stay by the teacher?		

Investigating Playtime — Map Work

One useful way for children to investigate playtime issues is through map work. On a simple plan of the school playground, children can record a variety of things.

For instance, the maps can be use to:

☐ Specify which games/activities are played where and who plays them

☐ Mark the area they best and least like to be at playtime

☐ Time sample usage over a playtime (see example 1).

☐ 'Track' (follow) one child during playtime, marking their path (see example 2).

☐ Mark which areas of the playground are sunny, shady, windy, dark etc.

☐ Mark where helpers stand

Time Sample of Lunch Play

Example 1

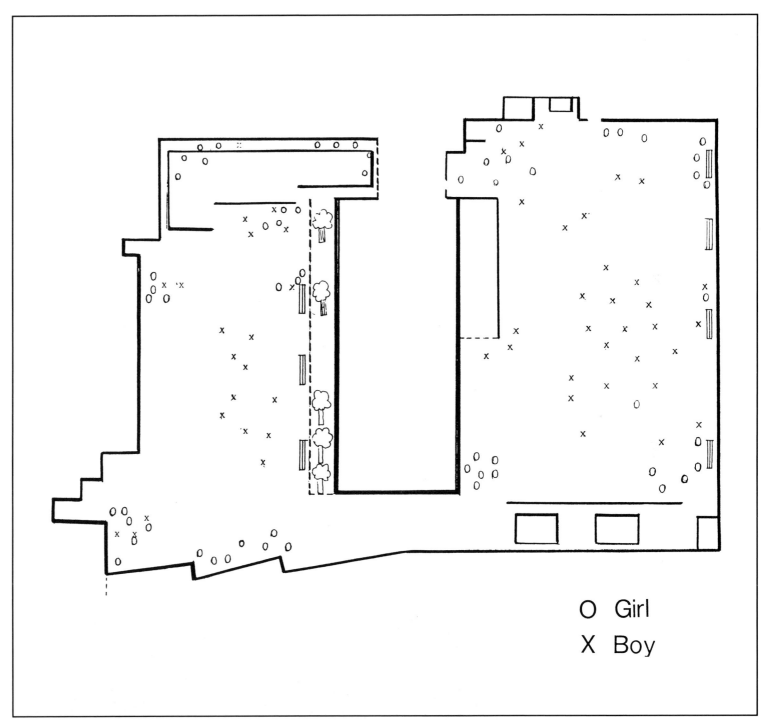

O Girl

X Boy

'Tracking' an
Infant Boy, Aged 6

Example 2

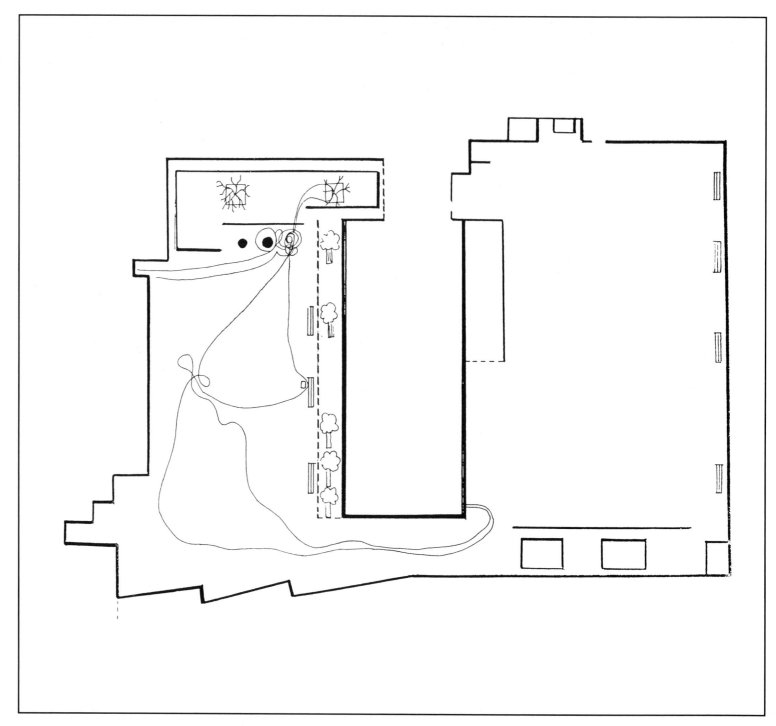

Developing Map Work Further — Fair Shares

This activity is designed to reveal whether the play space is fairly shared. It can serve as a basis for discussion about re-structuring usage. One school for example subsequently reduced the size of the football pitch.

1. From a plan of the playground, the children calculated the total available area.

2. The area is then divided by the number of pupils in the school to calculate each child's equal share.

3. An individual space allowance is chalked out in the playground. Children take turns standing inside.

4. The resulting discussion can be used to focus on:

   — sharing

   — use of space

   — inequalities

   — future changes

   — rules

Making A Playground Contract

It is beneficial to engage children in negotiating playground 'ground rules'. A 'contract-making' procedure works well for this:

1   Brainstorm sessions "What rules do we need on the playground?"

2   From these ideas select key issues and write on slips of paper.

3   Children arrange these slips in priority of importance (individually).

4   In small groups, children compare and discuss their ideas.

5   Share ideas as a whole class and come to a consensus. This is written down as the basis for creating a playground contract.

6   The final contracts should arise from a similar process with all classes and consultation with supervisors, teachers, etc.

Exploring Playground Issues as part of Curriculum Work

Much more can be done as part of classroom activities. Those below are some we've found effective.

- ☐ Keeping a diary of playtime experiences
- ☐ Creative writing around playtime issues
- ☐ Drama and role play
- ☐ Preparing an assembly
- ☐ Book making around collecting international games, skipping rhythms, etc.
- ☐ Drawing, painting, model making
- ☐ Photography (recording experience, starting points for discussion, role plays)
- ☐ Measuring the playground to produce an accurate map to scale
- ☐ History project exploring how playgrounds have changed.

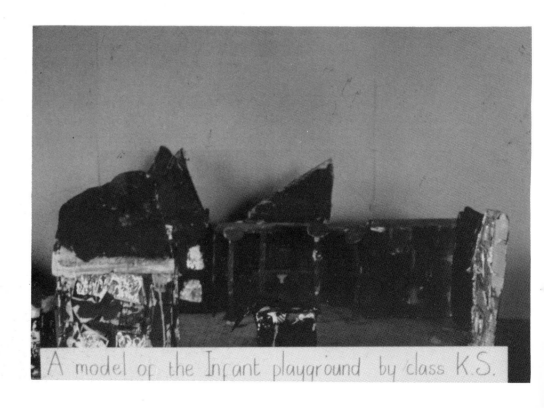

A model of the Infant playground by class K.S.

SECTION 3: Involving The Whole School Community

Playground issues effect everyone within the school community. In order to make effective changes, everyone must be involved in a relevant way. In this section, we consider ways of involving the various groups, communication, holding meetings, and ways of working together. We include a few examples of ways that schools have involved their community.

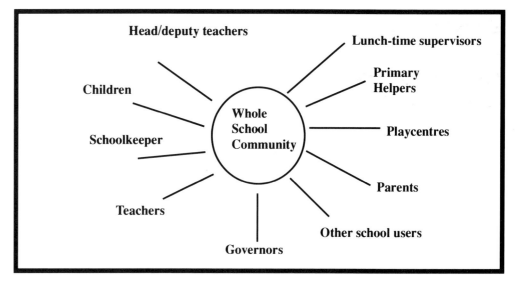

Head/deputy teachers

Lunch-time supervisors

Primary Helpers

Children

Whole School Community

Playcentres

Schoolkeeper

Parents

Teachers

Other school users

Governors

Strategy Plan

Playground Initiative: Work with the Whole Community

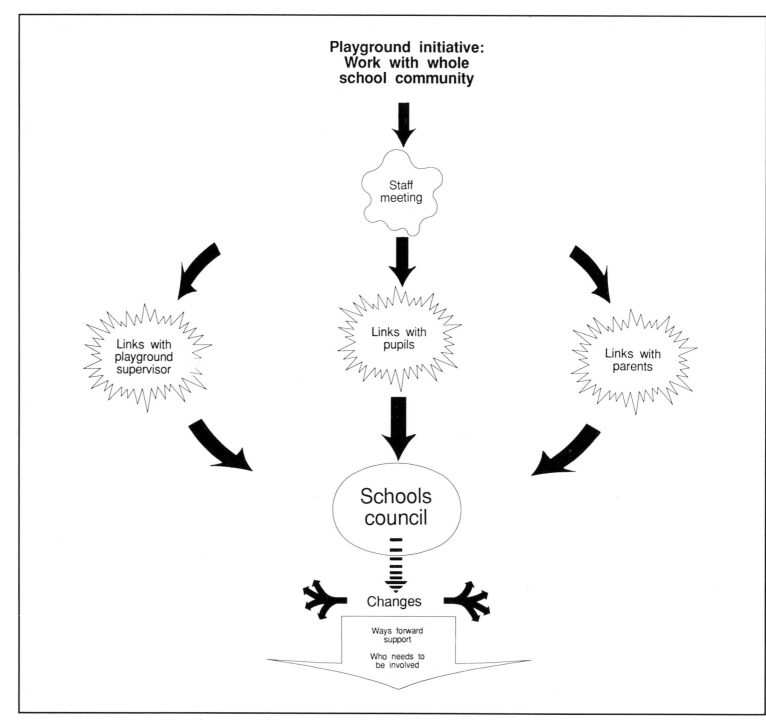

Strategies for Involving the School Community and Sharing Ideas

Although the ideal may be whole school meetings and workshops, these are rarely possible. Here are suggestions for some ways that schools can be moving forward over playground issues, even when there is little opportunity to discuss things together:

☐ Sharing incidents, issues, strategies etc. with one teaching colleague, but on a regular basis

☐ Establishing a link between one teacher and one dinner-time supervisor to share observations and feelings

☐ Establishing a small 'Informal Action Research Group': — a network of interested people identifying issues and working towards strategies. (For example it could comprise a teacher, a dinner-time supervisor and 2 pupils).

☐ A very specific aspect of the playground taken on as a whole school (or class) project (eg a 'human rights' project relating to children's rights (and staff's) on the playground; developing a quiet area; cooperative games)

☐ Practising conflict resolution with children in the classroom (e.g. through role play)

☐ Assemblies on playground issues, to share surveys etc.

☐ Producing a newsletter, to update progress

☐ A playground notice board — A place where people can put up comments, work done with pupils, progress reports, issues that need raising etc.

☐ Mounting a display based on classroom work on the playground

☐ Questionnaires

☐ Monitoring the playground (by pupils, teachers and/or helpers)

☐ Gaining recognition by establishing an official working party

☐ Making issues visible — for example:

a record of complaints from parents/from helpers/from pupils

a diary (or tick list) of problems from playtime that carry over into the classroom afterwards

☐ Inviting in outside advisors

☐ Brief regular slot in staff meetings to share ideas and practice or to report back on playground work.

☐ Parents' meeting/social/open evening

☐ Role play/drama

☐ Class meeting for pupils with agendas on playground matters

☐ Changes in rules/organisation monitored and shared

☐ Different groups within the school community meeting, separately or together

☐ Report-backs to governors' meetings

☐ Using the schools council to focus on and develop playground work

☐ Forming a playground committee.

Planning Meetings

Working with the whole school community will inevitably involve a series of meetings about different aspects of the project and be aimed at various groups. It is important that these meetings are organised in such a way as to encourage participation and be to maximum effect.

Considerations

Physical aspects —
☐ Seating arrangement (eg a circle will allow everyone to see each other)

☐ venue — (comfortable?)

Scheduling
☐ for convenience (e.g. staff meetings in school time)

☐ ample notification

Purpose
☐ Is the meeting necessary? (Will a letter do as well?)

☐ Are participants aware of the purpose?

☐ Introduction at beginning of meeting should re-state the purpose

Format
☐ Speaker? Workshop?

☐ Should be known to participants

Structuring a meeting so everyone can participate
☐ Opening 'ice-breaker' or 'warm up' (to create relaxed atmosphere and set the tone)

☐ Working in pairs/small groups (allows everyone to join in; less intimidating to speak up; avoids a few dominating the meeting)

☐ Alternating groups/pairs (allows people to meet/work with a variety of people)

☐ Devising tasks/activities (which allow groups/pairs to use as a basis for discussing an issue, devising a strategy)

☐ 'Energiser' — Midway activity to change the pace

☐ Group work/workshops can help build a 'sense of team'

Prioritising the agenda
☐ This ensures that important items aren't rushed or left out

Recording the minutes
☐ This can be done by an individual making notes later circulated or on a flip chart/blackboard as you go along

Review/ways forward/Next Step
☐ At conclusion of meeting

Rapid feedback from previous meeting

This page was written in collaboration with Pete Saunders (ILEA Advisor for Primary PSHE)

CHECKLIST FOR PREPARING AN AGENDA

1. What is the purpose(s) of the meeting?

2. What end results do you want/need from the meeting?

3. Who has called the meeting?

4. Who is invited to it?

5. Support facilities for the meeting (eg access, crèche...)

6. 'Rules of Conduct' — smoking etc.

7. Timing of the meeting

   — start

   — finish

   — breaks

   — timing of agenda items

8. Information: what should go on the agenda?

   what should go with it — reports, minutes...?

9. Prioritising the agenda according to importance or urgency

10. Are agenda items clear...well written, jargon-free, no abbreviations?

11. AOB — try and ensure notice is given of items before the meeting

12. Date of future meeting (s)

Identifying Targets

In order for the whole school community to work effectively, specific targets need to be identified. It can be difficult to know where to start on a playground project when there are so many issues and so many people involved. By brainstorming the range of work to be done, schools we worked with were able to identify specific goals. Individuals or groups within the school were then able to choose targets and develop strategies around them. Here are some targets that were identified.

Games:
Developing non-competitive games
(Work with pupils/workshops for teachers and supervisors)
Meeting, games from around the world
(Developing a reference library)
Play equipment — Fixed
Play equipment — Loose

Restructuring Play Space
Zoning for different play areas
Timetabling use
Developing a specific zone

Enhancing the Play Space
Art projects
Planting gardens

Monitoring the Playground
By pupils/by supervisors
Usage/Opinions/Experiences

Involving Parents
Views/support

Fundraising

Contract making/Rules
Consultation processes with
pupils/parents/supervisors/teachers

Procedures
Clear guidelines for enforcing
playground rules

Non-teaching staff
Introducing new equipment and games
Organising a system for loose
equipment loans

Schools Council/ Playground Committee

Schools with established school councils use these as a forum to involve the whole school community in their playground projects. Setting up a Playground Committee is another way schools have developed their playground initiatives. Such a committee or council should have representatives from the teaching staff, pupils, supervisors, parents, the school management and the caretaker.

It provides a means of promoting links and communication as well as coordinating different aspects and developments of a playground project. It can give an overview of the whole project and highlight ways forward.

In most schools working on playground change, there is a lot of on-going work on different levels — in the classroom, in staff meetings, by individual teachers, in meetings with parents or supervisors, with outside advisors, in terms of fund-raising and in relation to developing anti-racist and anti-sexist policies. It is important to ensure that all this work is complementary and developmental in that it builds on each initiative.

Working With Parents

Our research indicates that playground-related incidents are the main reason for informal visits of parents to primary schools. Parents we interviewed expressed a great deal of concern over what happens on the playground.

A common theme was the reluctance of their children to come to school because of problems on the playground, such as fighting, bullying, exclusion, name calling. Parents also voiced anxiety over the lack of structure in this part of the school day. There was a feeling that 'anything could happen'. There was also a good deal of worry over what their children are 'learning' on the playground, such as 'bad language'. Parents often described their dilemma in giving their children conflicting messages of: 'don't fight' and 'stand up for yourself'. Racist name calling was identified as a major problem. A frequent comment was that there was little to do other than play football.

It is important to find ways of involving parents in the school's playground project and sharing information about progress and policy; giving the opportunity to air views; exchanging ideas; engaging support. Here are some ideas from schools we've worked with:

- ☐ Inviting parents to assemblies about the playground
- ☐ PTA meetings on the playground
- ☐ Forming a playground committee with parent representation
- ☐ Newsletter home
- ☐ Questionnaires and interviews
- ☐ Pupils devising role plays around playground incidents/issues and inviting parents to see these 'performed'
- ☐ Parents meeting about the playground
- ☐ Agreeing with parents a set of procedures for dealing with unacceptable behaviour on the playground.

Workshop With Parents

Here is an example of a workshop with parents from one school. It used 'quote cards' as a trigger to stimulate discussion. These cards were devised from a series of interviews we held with parents from various schools:

1 Individually —

read through the cards and add your own statements to the blank cards.

2 In pairs —

rank the cards in the order which reflects your own concerns

3 In Fours —

share ideas with another pair and discuss

4 As a whole group

feedback from group discussions and documenting main issues.

The 'quote cards' follow.

Quote Cards

Cut into cards. Be sure to include several blanks so parents can add their own statements.

"The little ones are scared to come to school because of the playground"	"There's such a long lunchtime with nothing to do (except football)"
"Incidents that start in the classroom explode in the playground"	"Anything can hapen on the playground"
"The playground seems to be the most important experience to my children"	"Playtime is geared towards the boys — girls are left out"
"My son copes by making himself rougher and tougher"	"My kids don't tell anybody when they're bullied and called names"
"I don't know whether to tell my children not to fight or to tell them to stand up for themselves"	"I'm sure all the racism on the playground is at odds with school policy"
"The helpers don't seem to have any status to enforce the playground rules"	"Incidents on the playground are the main reason why I come in to school"

Lunchtime Supervisors

Lunchtime supervisors play a major role in the day to day running of the playground. Here are some issues which were identified in schools we've worked with. They raise central questions concerning the role of the supervisor within the school community. Use them as a basis for exploring and developing the role of lunchtime supervisors in your school.

Communication link with parents

☐ Supervisors often live locally and see parents and children outside of school. They may be more immediately accessible to parents than teachers. Parent-supervisor exchange can become an informal but important way for parents to communicate and also a way of promoting parental involvement in the school.

Communication with teachers

☐ Supervisors are aware of children's experiences and behaviour over the lunch hour. Establishing time for them to report back to teachers could provide valuable insights and important information about various children. This should not just be in terms of crisis situations.

How supervisors regard their role

☐ Many supervisors see their main priority as ensuring the safety of children in the playground. What other expectations are placed on them? Are these realistic?

Status of the supervisor

☐ How do the children regard the supervisor? How is their status perceived? What are the procedures and back-up within the school for dealing with playground conflict? How does the status of part-time and full time supervisors differ?

Supervisors are educationalists

☐ Support (eg workshops, training, resources, planning and meeting time) could help supervisors develop their role as facilitators of educational play.

Workshop Ideas for Playground Supervisors

The following workshop ideas have been used in schools to promote discussion among playground supervisors.

I. Mapping the Playground

Aims: to identify the issues surrounding lunchtime supervision of the playground

Individually:

Do a sketch of the playground

☐ Mark in resources
☐ Indicate trouble spots
☐ Usage (by whom? how? activities?)
☐ Mark in places where you stand
☐ Identify where you like/dislike to be

Compare and discuss your observations

II. Discussing Issues

Use the 'quote cards' to stimulate discussion and raise issues. Add your own comments to the blanks. The quotations are taken from interviews with playground supervisors.

"My main concern is about the safety of the children"	"Winter is a problem. The children get so cold and hate being outside"
"Our role as helpers is like being a mother — we have to do a lot of scolding and comforting"	"A lot of problems on the playground come from children being excluded"
"It's easier for us because we're full-time primary helpers and the children really get to know us well. The helpers who are just here at lunchtime find it more difficult"	"It's hard for the little ones — they are often overwhelmed by the older children. They just want to stay by you and hold on to you"
"Some children get upset or wound-up during lunch-time play. It might help the teachers if they knew what had happened"	"Parents don't like to bother the teachers in the morning but they will often ask us to keep an eye on their children if they're worried or their child's been poorly"

Supervisor's Playground Checklist

This checklist has been used by playground supervisors to monitor playtimes.

WHO IS *MAINLY* DOING THIS? (Please tick)	Girls	Boys	Both
Football			
Skipping			
Small ball games			
Sitting and chatting			
Hanging around adults			
Running			
Name-calling			
Interfering with smaller/weaker children			
Fighting			
Arguing			
Rudeness to adults			
Provoking trouble			
At a glance, who is using most of the playground space?			

SECTION 4: Changes to the Physical Playground

Changes To The Physical Playground

Playtime is the 'unstructured' part of the school day.

Many school playgrounds are simply empty areas where children are essentially left to their own devices. Problems that arise at playtime are often related to the use of the physical space. For instance:

1   The domination of space by one group and activity (such as football)

2   The lack of any clear boundaries between activities

3   The lack of a variety of activities.

Playtime should offer children the opportunity of undirected play whereby they can develop socially, physically and creatively. A well structured play-space offers children a variety of experiences.

Playtime can then become about the freedom to make choices from a range of activities rather than about confusion generated by the 'freedom' of a chaotic unstructured playground.

This section suggests ideas for structuring the playspace ('zoning') and developing specific areas ('zones').

As well as more major projects, effective changes to the playground can be made on a small or temporary scale. Trialing changes on a small scale can also be valuable in planning larger scale changes.

Games, rules, procedures and policies should be developed alongside physical changes to the playground. We discuss these in the next section.

Creating Zones In The Playground

Different school communities will have different zoning needs and priorities. It's up to each school to decide what zones they want to have in their playground. Here are some ideas for zones that have been chosen by schools we've worked with:

- ☐ Garden area
- ☐ Area for loose equipment (e.g. ropes, small balls, small toys...)
- ☐ Quiet Area
- ☐ Fixed play equipment
- ☐ Informal activity area (e.g. chase games)
- ☐ Area with playground markings (e.g. set games like hopscotch)

For each zone, there are a range of considerations involving location, usage and organisation.

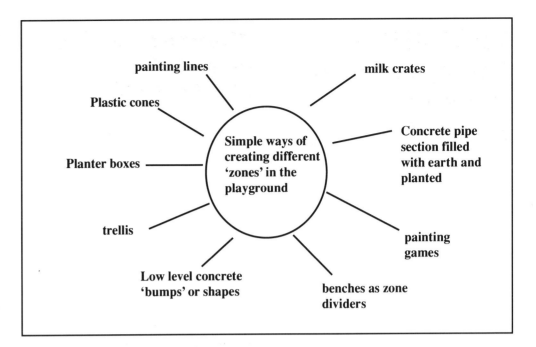

Simple ways of creating different 'zones' in the playground

- painting lines
- Plastic cones
- Planter boxes
- trellis
- Low level concrete 'bumps' or shapes
- milk crates
- Concrete pipe section filled with earth and planted
- painting games
- benches as zone dividers

Creating a zone with painted markings

Creating a zone using benches and planter tubs

Zoning —
A Sample Plan for
the Development
of the Playground

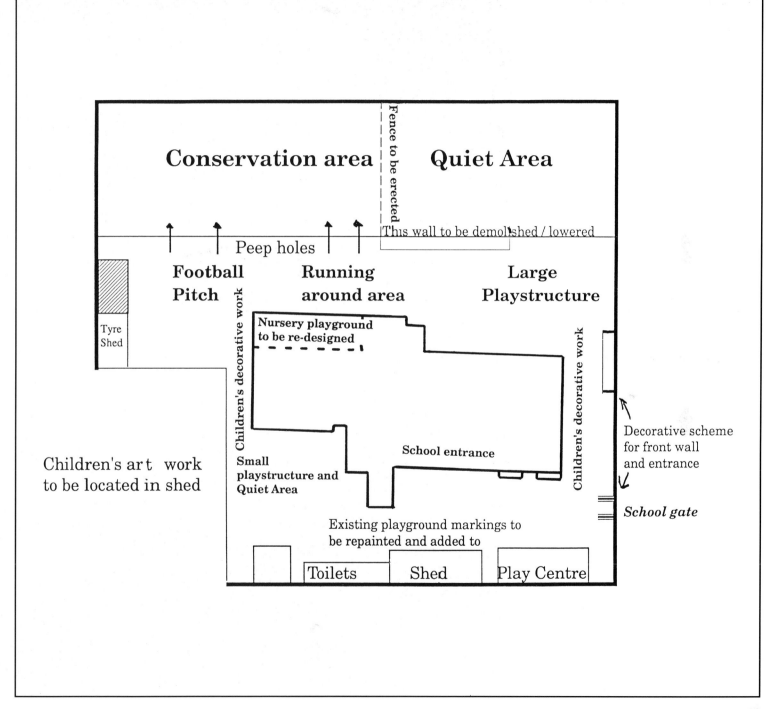

Conservation area

Quiet Area

Fence to be erected

Peep holes

This wall to be demolished / lowered

Football
Pitch

Running
around area

Large
Playstructure

Children's decorative work

Nursery playground
to be re-designed

Children's decorative work

Tyre
Shed

Children's art work
to be located in shed

Small
playstructure and
Quiet Area

School entrance

Decorative scheme
for front wall
and entrance

School gate

Existing playground markings to
be repainted and added to

Toilets

Shed

Play Centre

Considerations for zoning the playground

What physical changes will be necessary?

What are your special needs groups?

What equipment is needed?

What kind of parental support is needed? (Fund-raising? Consultation?)

What are the drainage requirements?

What are the access issues? (Fire engines, grounds maintainance)

How many children must be catered for?

What are the maintainance requirements?

What on-going method of monitoring usage will be neeed?

Rules

How can we ensure equal usage?

Considerations for zones in the Playground

What are the health and safety issues?

What practical ways are there of dividing up space?

How will supervision needs change?

How will changes affect current use?

Are there existing structures?

What are the needs of other users?

Where are the sunny areas?

What funds are available?

What range of activities will be on offer?

What is the size, shape and area of available space?

What are the potential problems?

Will timetabling be required?

Considering Each Zone

Here are some points to consider when setting up the various 'zones' in your playground.

Garden Area

Usage

☐ Teacher-directed (curriculum-related)

☐ As a quiet play area

☐ For school events

Benefits

☐ As an educational resource

☐ Oasis in a concrete jungle

☐ Conservation area

Possible problems

☐ Maintenance — who will look after it?

☐ Who will supervise it?

☐ Health and Safety/trees and plants must be chosen with care (no poisonous berries)

☐ If it contains water it will need to be supervised/protected at all times

Rules

☐ An agreement as to its use — the care of the plants etc.

☐ If there is to be grass, agreement as to when it can be used

☐ Behaviour expected in this area

Strategies to give everybody a chance

☐ Timetabling

☐ Specific areas of responsibility

Practical ideas for setting up

☐ Existing planting or grass area could be extended and developed

☐ Parents might give their labour to reduce costs

☐ Seating/tables can extend usage

☐ A container garden could provide a cheap alternative to digging up the playground

Fixed Play Equipment

Usage
- [ ] Active Play
- [ ] Focus for imaginative play.
- [ ] A meeting place

Benefits
- [ ] Develops physical skills
- [ ] An alternative to ordinary playground space
- [ ] Provides different levels and viewpoints for more varied play opportunities
- [ ] Can be used individually or in groups.

Possible problems
- [ ] The equipment will need a safety surface, and regular safety checks
- [ ] Maintenance will be required
- [ ] It will need to be supervised to prevent domination by one group
- [ ] It may increase accidents if improperly used — or not introduced sensibly
- [ ] Inappropriate footwear and clothing could be problems
- [ ] Could accentuate gender differences.

Rules
- [ ] An awareness of the number of people who can use it safely
- [ ] An agreed code of behaviour amongst the children and helpers as to the safe use of the equipment.

Strategies to give everyone a chance
- [ ] Timetable by class, age, gender
- [ ] Use in P.E. lessons/groups or girl only time to give confidence and extend possibilities.

Practical Ideas for setting up
- [ ] May need to be set up around existing structures
- [ ] New equipment could be expensive
- [ ] A structure could provide the added function of breaking up the playspace.

Playground Markings

Usage

- [ ] Traditional set games — hopscotch, king ball etc.
- [ ] Inventing new games

Benefits

- [ ] New painted markings could be open-ended (e.g. circle markings) for imaginative play or new games
- [ ] Suitable for individual or group play
- [ ] Provides an active game within a structured space

Possible problems

- [ ] Can be competitive/exclusive
- [ ] Can be easily disrupted

Rules

- [ ] Agreement about turn-taking and not disrupting games in progress

Practical ideas for setting up

- [ ] Choose a quiet area of the playground to avoid disruptions of games
- [ ] Involve the children in designing new games
- [ ] Initiate new games that allow flexibility, *This can be done by the children.*

Formal Games Pitch

Usage

☐ Variety of games in lesson time as well as playtime

Benefits

☐ Develops physical and team skills
Gives structure to play

☐ A chance to engage in active play

Possible problems

☐ Conflict over who gets to play

☐ Conflict within the play

☐ Domination by one group or game

☐ Over competitiveness

☐ Exclusion of children who aren't very skilled

☐ Encroaches on other areas

Rules

☐ Timetabling/rota system of games and players

☐ Definite boundaries to the pitch

☐ Agreed rules for playing

Strategies to give everybody a chance

☐ Work in class time to develop skills

☐ Timetabling by class group, age, gender

☐ A weekly session which is bookable by groups of children

Practical ideas for setting up

☐ The pitch needs to be contained by existing walls, corners, placing benches or siting panels or trellis to prevent the game dominating the whole play space, the balls escaping and the size of the pitch growing. This would also help to break up the whole space and create a protected space for another activity.

Informal Active Area

Usage
- [ ] Chase games, imaginative and pretend games

Benefits
- [ ] An opportunity for the children to engage in undirected play.
- [ ] Entrance not determined by skills or equipment
- [ ] Flexible — ever changing

Possible problems
- [ ] A group could develop a sense of ownership and then be unwilling to share the space
- [ ] The space could become very rough under the guise of being active and a free choice area

Rules
- [ ] Rules for safe use of the space, sharing, what happens when someone is hurt etc. must be agreed
- [ ] Allow time out from playtime to talk about what went on and any grievances

Quiet Area

Usage

- [ ] Sitting, chatting, story-telling, drama, reading, board games, drawing

Quiet Play

- [ ] Provides a protected area away from more physical/noisy activities of the playground

Possible problems

- [ ] Will need supervision
- [ ] Could be vulnerable to invasion by outside games
- [ ] Needs to be a high status attractive area of the playground, a positive choice not a sanctuary.

Rules

- [ ] No running through the area
- [ ] No equipment taken from the loose equipment area

Strategies to give everybody a chance

- [ ] Make the area/seating appropriate to the number of children in the school and the other activities on offer.
- [ ] Give classes priority usage on a timetabled basis

Practical ideas for setting up

- [ ] Could be an arrangement of benches and planter tubs in a sunny spot in the playground
- [ ] Needs to be sited or screened by trellis, low wall, benches away from noisy or dominant physical activities like football.
- [ ] Alternatively, it could be indoors.

Area for Loose Equipment

Usage

☐ For skipping games, two balls, marbles, hoops, toys from home...

Benefits

☐ Provides an alternative to running, chasing games

☐ Encourages cooperation between children — turn taking/sharing

☐ Develops skills — hand/eye coordination

Possible problems

☐ Fighting over equipment/sharing/turn taking

☐ Losing equipment

☐ Competition for space

Rules

☐ Agreement by children and system for sharing equipment and space

Strategies to give everybody a chance

☐ A rota for using the area — timetable priority times for classes

☐ A loan system for equipment

☐ Children could make simple toys to compensate for toys that got lost, broken, suffered wear and tear (e.g. Spinning tops, bean bags, puppets, can and strding stilts.)

Practical skills for setting up

☐ This area could combine with the playground markings area or informal games area

☐ Screening the area using planters and trellis would contain equipment within that area of the playground — making distribution, supervision and collection of equipment easier.

☐ A system of collecting equipment

☐ An accessible shed, cupboard, box or tray, supervised by children or helpers, would make collecting equipment easier.

Small Equipment Ideas

Small equipment can be useful on the playground for contained space/quiet areas or at wet play. These items are inexpensive and could be bought by the school for playtime.

- ☐ Spinning top
- ☐ plasticine
- ☐ cup and ball
- ☐ wooden spinner on a string
- ☐ jacks
- ☐ yo-yo
- ☐ straws
- ☐ marbles

- ☐ whipping top
- ☐ plastic hoops
- ☐ skipping ropes
- ☐ frisbee
- ☐ small balls
- ☐ boxes of farm animals
- ☐ boxes of miniture cars
- ☐ play bricks

Organising A loose Equipment Library

There needs to be a system for managing the distribution and collection of loose equipment. One way is to set up an 'equipment library' with a loans system (which children can be involved in running). There may need to be time limits during long lunch breaks. It can be organised on a whole school or a class-by-class basis. In order to be workable, the system must be one that 'runs itself'.

Booking form for loose equipment   *Sample*

Please fill in name

DATE	Morning break	Lunchtime break	Afternoon break	Returned please
Small rope				
Large rope				
Small ball				
Large Ball				
Hoop				
Bat				
Frisbee				
Marbles				
Whip and top				
Box of Miniture cars				
Play bricks				
Box of Farm Animals				

Monitoring Loose Equipment

Monitoring new equipment is a useful way to find out how it is being used, who is using it, how it's being shared, and identifying any problems that arise. This is an evaluation sheet we have used.

New Loose Equipment

Description of toy/activity/game

How was it introduced?

Who used it?

How was it distributed?

Was adult support necessary?

Any problems arising?

Children's responses?

Other comments?

Evaluating the Zones

Throughout the process of establishing zones in the playground, evaluation should be taking place to determine the next steps. This can be especially useful before making expensive changes to the physical playground. Here is an evaluation sheet we have found helpful.

Description of Zone (Activities, location...)	Usage (who and how?)	Organisation (Supervision equipment loan system, rates, rotas)	Comments

Developing a Zone

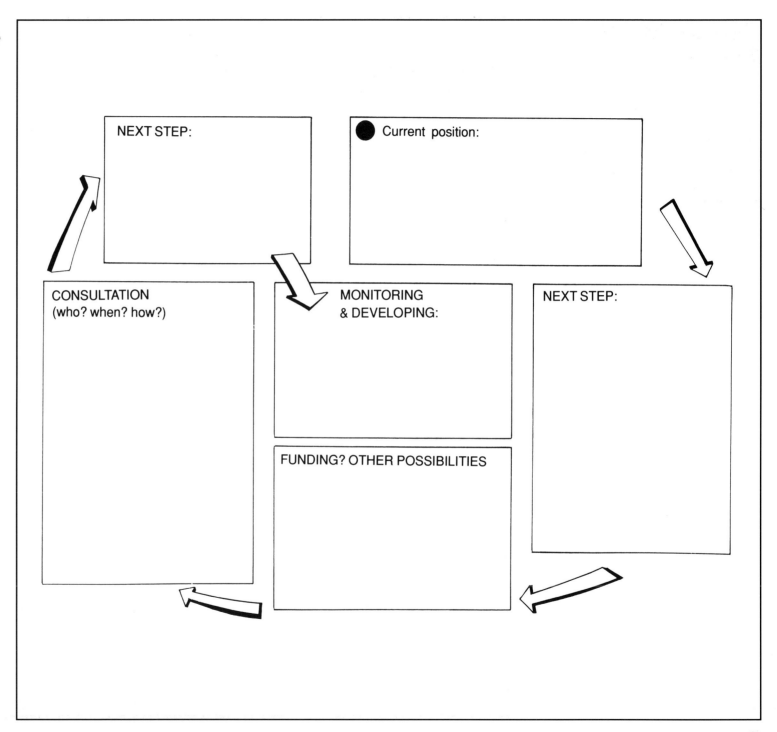

NEXT STEP:

Current position:

CONSULTATION
(who? when? how?)

MONITORING
& DEVELOPING:

NEXT STEP:

FUNDING? OTHER POSSIBILITIES

SECTION 5: Playground Strategies

Playground Strategies

Making changes to the playground not only involves altering the physical space but must also include developing positive strategies which relate to its use. This means creating systems that allow:

- [ ] play to be organised in a way that ensures equal access for all children
- [ ] the development of games and activities which promote cooperation
- [ ] the development of positive ways of dealing with conflict
- [ ] an agreed system of governing playtime.

This section looks specifically at developing positive strategies around these issues.

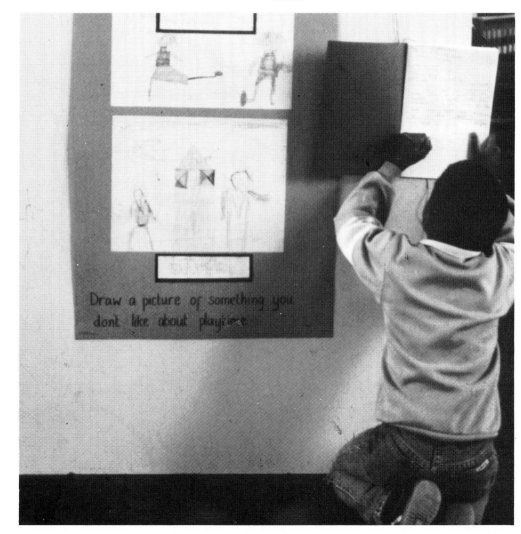

Timetabling for equal opportunity

Timetabling usage of space is a way to ensure that all children get a chance at all the activities. In the schools we have worked in, monitoring revealed a number of problematic situations which could be effectively addressed through timetabling.

The problems include —

☐ a group of boys dominating the active areas

☐ football the only game being played in the active area

☐ many girls and younger children marginalised to the edges of the playground and consequently their active play restricted

☐ certain children 'owning' certain areas and activities.

Timetabling Systems as strategies:

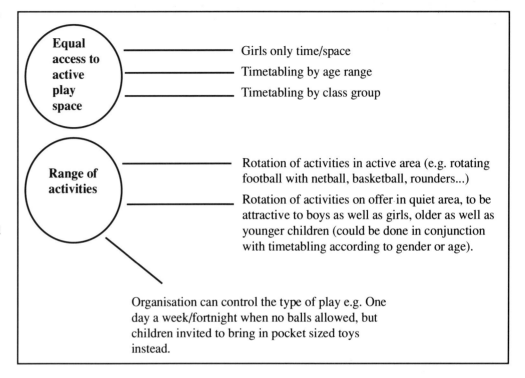

Equal access to active play space
- Girls only time/space
- Timetabling by age range
- Timetabling by class group

Range of activities
- Rotation of activities in active area (e.g. rotating football with netball, basketball, rounders...)
- Rotation of activities on offer in quiet area, to be attractive to boys as well as girls, older as well as younger children (could be done in conjunction with timetabling according to gender or age).

Organisation can control the type of play e.g. One day a week/fortnight when no balls allowed, but children invited to bring in pocket sized toys instead.

Rota for Use of the Games Pitch

Sample

	Morning	Lunchtime	Afternoon
Monday		Open	
Tuesday		Infant only time	
Wednesday		Open	
Thursday		Girl only time	
Friday		Open	Can be booked in advance

☐ Netball ☐ Football

☐ Hockey ☐ Cricket

☐ Rounders

Booking a Zone

Some schools allowed groups of children to book an area of the playground during one afternoon play session a week. Children used a booking form to reserve the area of their choice. This scheme allowed children to use the playground space in a range of ways, gave more children a chance to use areas of the playground they wouldn't normally use and exercise more control over their playtime

---

Quiet Area Booking Form

The area is available once a week for bookings from 12.15 to 1.15 pm.

Please allow 10 minutes for clearing up.

Name/s of group organiser/s _____

Number in group (up to 15) _____

What do you want to do _____

_____

_____

What facilities do you need (chairs, tables, chess board, pens etc.)

_____

_____

Who will be responsible for setting up _____

Who will be responsible for clearing away _____

Which day/date would you like to do this _____

1st Choice _____

2nd Choice _____

3rd Choice _____

Promoting Cooperation through play

Fostering cooperative play helps to reduce conflict on the playground. Introducing cooperative games has been an important element in many schools' playground projects. Organisations and books are available which give ideas for collaborative games. (Some of these are listed in the Further Reading section.) Here are some points which have been found useful about introducing new games.

Introducing a new cooperative game:

☐ Build up the components of the game slowly. Give one rule first, allowing time for it to be practised. Then introduce the next rule.

☐ When children see the game running on its own without teacher direction, they find it easier to transfer it into the playground. After learning the game, children could be split into groups to practice running it themselves.

☐ Zoning the playground can create protected areas for circle/cluster games/fantasy games

☐ Some games can be rehearsed in the classroom

☐ Games where everybody does something at the same time avoid putting any one child on the spot

☐ Develop a built-in strategy to avoid any child being the one who isn't 'chosen'.

Managing the group

☐ Children's interaction can be controlled by the way the game is arranged.
e.g. When there is an 'unpopular' child:
a) structure the game so that they are automatically selected
b) create a 'safe' situation in which to select the child as 'it'.

Rules

Basic rules are needed to ensure that all can join in, and that no-one is hurt or 'spoils' the game.

This page written in collaboration with Carry Gourney (InterAction).

Conflict Resolution (Vs Damage Limitation)

Resolving conflict is a major playground issue

Conflict resolution techniques are based on the belief that good relationships depend on efficient communication, a cooperative atmosphere, and affirmation of the value of each individual. Identifying and practising these skills allows for the growth of trust and security, enabling children to explore techniques for analysing conflict and suggesting constructive solutions.

The activity on the following two pages has been devised by Tom Leimdorfer (Education Advisor, Quaker Peace and Service) and Sue Bowers (Director of Kingston Friends Workshop Group). It revolves around a playground incident: it gives four different perspectives. It aims to allow participants the opportunity to analyse a conflict situation and practise mediation.

Mediating conflict should be regarded as a process rather than a single solution:

Mediating Conflict

stages of problem solving:

1. Children relating only to the problem/incident

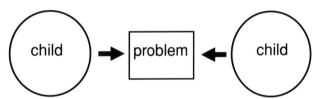

2. The teacher/supervisor needs to help the children to define the problem in a simple and purely descriptive way

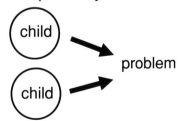

3. The children can then be helped to relate to each other and work towards a practical resolution

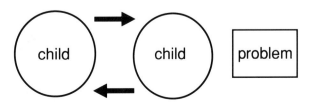

Analysing conflict

Here are four people who are involved, directly or indirectly, in an incident in the playground. In groups of four, take a role each and try to identify how each person sees the incident. Write down the main issues to share with other groups.

A BOY

You are late going out to the playground because teacher talked to you at the end of the class and then you had to go to the toilet. By the time you get out there, they have already picked sides for a game of football and they tell you that you are too late to join in. You try to join in anyway, but the others get cross and send you away. You don't fancy climbing on the apparatus because it looks full of children who are very noisy and mainly bigger than you. A couple of girls are playing skipping nearby. As one hands the rope to the other, you snatch it on impulse. They shout at you to hand it back, but you run round the corner and hide it in the 'scary bushes'. The girls get very angry and, when you reappear, they start calling you nasty names and follow you. You grab the hair of one of them and kick her. She screams. The dinner lady shouts at you to stop immediately and to come over to her. You are very upset and start to cry.

B GIRL

You are playing a skipping game with your friend. As she hands the rope back for your turn, a boy snatches it from you. This is the second time your game has been interupted and you yell at him angrily to give it back, but he runs away with it round the corner. You both run after him and just see him disappear into the 'scary bushes'. You don't like to follow him there because a group of bigger boys are playing a game rushing in and out. When he reappears, the skipping rope is nowhere to be seen. Both you and your friend are very angry and demand that he brings it back, but he just walks away. You start to follow and start calling all the ugly names you can think of. He turns round, pulls your hair till it hurts and kicks you. You scream to attract the attention of the dinner lady.

C DINNER LADY

You are the dinner-time playground supervisor. It has not been your day and you were a minute or two late. The children seem even noisier than usual and your attention is drawn to the apparatus where too many children are trying to climb on at the same time and you are afraid that some smaller children may get pushed off. You walk to the apparatus and tell some of them to get off and come back later. As you walk round the corner you hear a loud scream and see a boy pulling a girl's hair and looking as if he is trying to kick her. You yell at him to stop and come to you. By the time he gets to you he is in tears: 'They called me nasty names, Miss!'. The two girls speak at once: 'He's spoilt our game!' — 'He took our skipping rope!'. The situation on the apparatus looks dangerous again, so you march the boy and the girl who was kicked, off to the staffroom, demand rather crossly that the boy should be severely dealt with, and return hurriedly to sort out the apparatus.

D TEACHER

You had quite a good morning with your class. Everyone seemed fully involved with the activity you planned and you were particularly pleased that one lad, who is a bit of a loner, joined in so well with the others in his group. You kept him behind for a minute or two just to give him an encouraging word. As you settle to your sandwiches in the staffroom, there is an urgent knock on the door. You are surprised to find the same lad there in tears and accompanied by a very flushed looking girl from the parallel class and the dinner supervisor who is clearly flustered and is demanding instant retribution for the boy. She rushes away, saying that she must see to some other children. So far you have a garbled story with the girl complaining about kicking, hair-pulling and a missing skipping rope and the boy complaining about name calling, but also muttering something about 'them' shooing him away from football.

Stages of Problem Soving

In your four roles, discuss these questions, with the teacher as mediator.

Four questions for problem solvers:
What happened/what is the problem? (The teacher may need to interpret and feed back — a brief description is being sought, e.g. 'There was a disagreement on the playground and it's not solved'.)

How do you feel about it? (This may need to be heard separately from each person involved.)

What do you wish would happen? (How each person would like to see the problem resolved.)

What could you actually do? (Identify options — work towards a practical solution.)

Governing Playtime

Devising a system for governing playtime should ensure that all children have equal play opportunities, are protected from harassment and are safe. There are three broad aspects to this system:

1. Identifying issues

2. Rule making

3. Rule enforcement

1. Identifying the Issues

The first stage is the identification of troublesome behaviour and trouble/danger spots — trying to pinpoint problems and difficulties. This needs to be done from the different perspectives of members of the school community. Ideas for clarifying concerns of pupils, supervisors, teachers and parents are dealt with in other sections of this book.

2. Rule making

There are different ways of organising the making of rules, based on the concerns identified in stage one. This is the way some schools have worked:

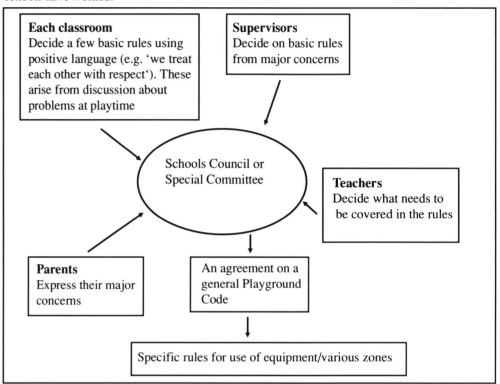

3. Enforcement

A set procedure is needed for enforcing the agreed playground code. Everyone needs to be clear about exactly what will happen; at what point parents are involved; warning systems; further sanctions; procedures between supervisors, teachers and headteachers.

In working out an effective system, other considerations might include:

☐ what happens if it is always the same children? What does this mean?

☐ is there a procedure for children to redeem themselves?

☐ is it necessary to make special allowance for certain children?

☐ do we build in a reward system?

☐ a system of review for effectiveness

☐ dealing with bad behaviour in more effective and positive ways

☐ focusing on activities or incidents rather than on individual children

Involving Parents

Parents need to be clear about playground rules and procedure. Here is an example of a letter sent to all parents in one school, informing them about the new code of conduct.

Dear Parents,

Here is our Playground Code:

1   We will always be kind and considerate to everybody in the playground

2   We will look after the playground and make sure that it is always a nice place to be in

3   We will share the playground space so that other games besides football can be played

4   Even if we are in the midst of something very exciting or important, we will stop and listen to any instructions an adult may give us.

It has been decided that serious breaking of the Code would mean the child's name being entered into a special book, and after three such entries, parents would be invited to the school to discuss their child's behaviour. An entry into the book could be a last resort and would be for behaviour such as:-

— running out of school

— abusive language to the responsible adult in the playground

— bullying, foul language etc. to other children.

We will 'launch' the Code at a whole school assembly, including playcentre, lunch time and kitchen staff and parents so that everyone in the school will know where they stand. We hope this will make the playground a better place for *everyone.*

There will be a review of progress of this project towards the end of half-term but in the meantime we would welcome any comments on this scheme that you might care to make.

The children have been involved with this project through classwork, discussions and the School's Council and we trust that you will feel able to give this Playground Code your full support.

Yours sincerely,

SECTION 6: Evaluating and Reviewing Progress

Reviewing Playground Projects

Reviewing is a key aspect of the teaching process in all school work. Through the process of questioning whether activities are enabling, productive and beneficial to the child's development, we as teachers are able to appraise the strengths of our methods. It is by identifying and learning from mistakes that creative changes take place.

Teachers are aware that the experiences in the playground, as well as in the classroom, are an important aspect of the school day. Evaluating playtime and collecting information about the experiences and feelings of playground users have to be an ongoing aspect of any playground project. Chats (informal interviews) with the following groups will provide some useful feedback:

i)   the children (a cross section, in terms of gender, ethnicity and age etc.)

ii)   playground supervisors

iii) parents (again a cross section)

iv)   other teachers

v)   relevant community groups

After collecting information and examining the points emerging, particular issues may be prioritised for further exploration. For instance if 'bullying is identified as a priority, the review might concentrate on finding out whether changes in playground policy really do reduce the number of bullying incidents.

Another important function of evaluation is to review the overall progress of the project. Drawing up a flow chart or action plan enables those involved to see what they have accomplished and what needs developing further. Reviewing as a collaborative process can lead to a sense of shared achievement and a resolve to do more.

Some initiatives will be more successful than others. What matters is that we define and acknowledge the learning that takes place through identifying our mistakes and making creative changes. Logging the process and responding to the outcomes and insights can support a whole school development plan in a practical way. That is what good evaluation is all about.

Using Evaluation to Help Implement Playground Initiatives

Evaluation can be a powerful factor in whole school development. It can involve taking into account the views of the whole school community and in making decisions and judgements about what is happening in the school. It can be a way to share concerns and ideas, disseminate strategies and initiatives and inform practice. Here are two interviewing techniques which can be helpful in evaluation work. The following pages describe two interviewing techniques helpful in evaluation, adapted here into worksheets to facilitate evaluating various stages of playground project.

This page written in collaboration with Gael Parfitt (ILEA Evaluation Consultant).

Interviewing

I: Co-Counselling as an Evaluation Technique

Co-counselling can be used as a technique for interviewing and reviewing. It provides a way of structuring an interview so that power relationships do not interfere.

Confidentiality must be established — what is to be shared with the school and what is private. It is possible to share the general issues or concerns while still maintaining anonymity.

Co-counselling can be used as a focused time to share ideas about a specified issue or area of practice. By logging the issues arising from these sessions, they become informal interviews which can be used as evaluation research or as a means of disseminating ideas and practice.

Method Of Co-counselling

a)   Structure

Participants-directed: participants determine the content, rate and depth of work; they specify the contract determining what counselling interventions are acceptable; they can reject counselling interventions; they can make their own interventions.

Equal time: in every session the time is halved and each person spends half the time in the interviewer's role and half as the interviewee.

b)   **Types of Contracts**

the participants specify the contract at the beginning of the sessions:-

free attention: interviewer gives non-verbal support only.

normal: interviewer intervenes if the interviewee appears stuck, in pattern, or to be missing their own cues

intensive: interviewer uses every cue to encourage the interviewee.

II: Interviewing activity (in threes)

1.   Chat about school issues

2.   Work out a set of six questions

3.   Interview each other on these questions with one person as interviewer, one as interviewee and one as observer.

Interview each other on more questions (with one person as interviewer, one as interviewee and one as observer):

Starting to Analyse Playground Issues

1. What are the main issues you've identified about the playground?

2. Which area/areas you've prioritised would it be useful to explore further or involve other people at school in looking at?

3. What ideas do you have for monitoring or taking things forward?

At What Stage is Your Playground Project?

Structure and Organisation for example: Girls only time/space, Staggered playtimes, Quiet alternatives, Indoor times, No Football Other	
Positive Strategies on the Playground for example: Conflict resolution (damage limitation/long term strategies), Positive approaches to discipline, Rules and Procedures, Cooperative games etc. Other	
Working with pupils for example: About name calling, About fighting and bullying, Group work, Discussions	
Monitoring ideas and techniques	
Involving Parents for example: meetings, letters, inviting them in	
Whole School Community for example: developments, communication processes, schools council	
Evaluation and Dissemination of Ideas	
Physical Changes to the Playground (large or small)	
Fund Raising	

Playground Initiatives — Deciding the next step

Describe stage by stage the steps taken in your school towards changing the playground:

1 a) please give a clear description of any monitoring

b) How did it go? Any difficulties? Interesting outcomes? Other developments?

c) What will be your next step?

2 a) Who in school community has been involved?

b) Describe how they have been involved (e.g. meetings , surveys, monitoring etc.)

c) What will be your next step?

3 a) Have any contacts been made outside school? (Who, how?)

b) What will be your next step?

Playground Initiatives Throughout the School

People/ Groups Involved	Meetings	Monitoring/ identifying issues	Conflict Resolution	Rules/ Contract making	Exploring strategies (e.g. Assertion Techniques)	Exploring Issues e.g. name calling	Other initiatives
Whole School							
Governors							
Outside Agencies							
Playcentre							
Parents							
Teaching staff							
Non-teaching staff							
Head/ Dept. head							
Classroom/ Pupils							
Playground changes	**Rules**	**Organisation**	**Design**	**Games/Play**	**Alternatives**	**Procedures**	**Other changes**

What is the next step?

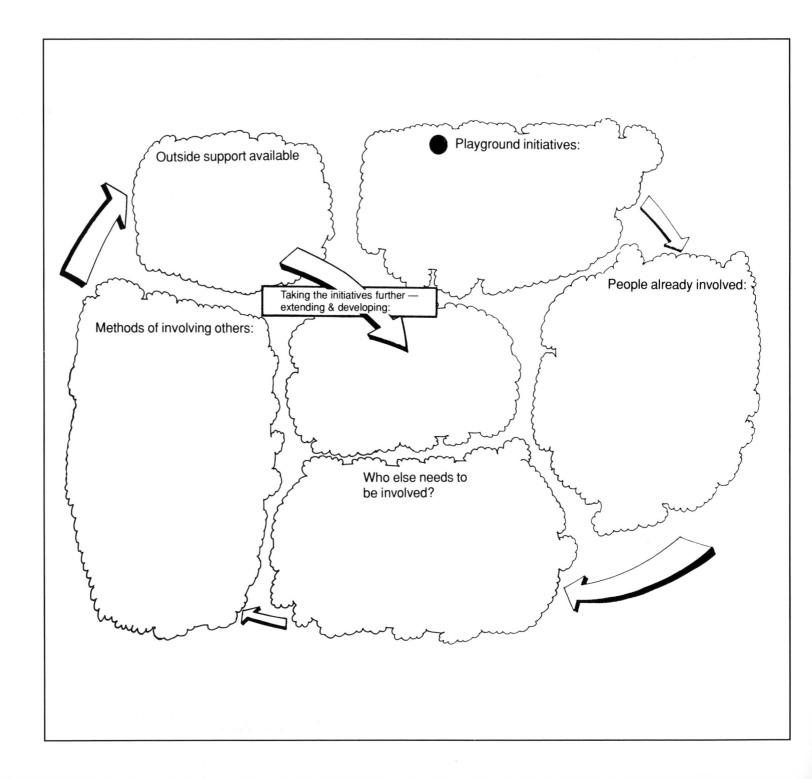

Outside support available

● Playground initiatives:

Taking the initiatives further — extending & developing:

Methods of involving others:

People already involved:

Who else needs to be involved?

Action Plan

What is to be done	How it is to be done	By when (Date)	Person Responsible	Possible Problems

Further Reading

Cooperative Games

BRANDES D.: **Gamesters Handbook** (1 and 2) Hutchinson 1987.

INTERACTION: **Game songs with Prof. Dogg's Troups** (with cassette) A. & C. Black.

MASHEDER M.: **Lets Cooperate** Peace Pledge Union 1986.

ORLICK T.: **The Cooperative Sports and Games Book** Pantheon 1978 **Challenge Without Competition.**

One Potato, two potato, a book about children's games A. & C. Black.

How do people play? Games from many lands MacDonald.

The Great Playtime Games Kit National Playing Fields Association, Orpington Square, London SW2 1LQ.

Playing for Life New Games, 11 Plato Road, London SW2.

The Physical Playground

ALLAN P.: **Playstructures — Participation and design** by children Community Service, Volunteers and The Islington Schools Environmental Project, 237 Pentonville Road, London N1 9NJ 1988.

FRIEDBERG P.: **Do It Yourself Playgrounds** The Architectural Press Ltd., London.

HESELTINE P and Holborn J.: **Playgrounds: the planning design and construction of play environments** Mitchell Press 1987.

HOGAN P.: **The Nuts and Bolts of Playground Construction: A Trilogy of Play** (Vol 1 to 3) Leisure Press, Phoenixville, Arizona.

MARES C. and STEPHENSON R.: **Inside Outside** Tidy Britain Group, Schools Research Project, Brighton Polytechnic.

MARTIN R.: **It's not all swings and roundabouts** Womens Design Service, 15 Wilkin Street, London NW5 3NG.

SONONON L.: **Making Playgrounds** Community Service Volunteers, 237 Pentonville Road, London N1 9NJ.

Playing Safe: a checklist for assessing children's playgrounds National Playing Fields Association, 25 Orpington Square, London SW2 1LQ.

Relative Issues

BARNET Y.: **Miss, girls don't like playing big games, they only like playing little games: Gender differences in the use of the playground** Primary Teaching Studies, Volume 4 Number 1, October 1988.

BLATCHFORD P.: **Girls and boys come out to play** Thomas Koram Unit, London Institute of Education 1988.

KELLY E. and COHN T.: **Racism in Schools: New Research Evidence** Trentham Books 1988.

SANDERS P.: **The School Playground** Child Education May 1987.

TATTUM D. and LANE D.W.: **Bullying in Schools** Trentham Books 1989.

WARD C.: **The Child in the City** Routledge, Kegan Paul.

Strategies

JUDSON S.: **A manual of non-violence and children** New Society Publishers 1984.

NICHOLAS F.M.: **Coping with conflict: A resource book for Middle School years** Learning Development Aids.

Ways and Means: an approach to problem solving Kingston Friends Workshop 1985.

Self Defence for Girls and Young Women Inner London Education Authority Equal Opportunities 1987.